Verses From The West Midlands

Edited By Holly Sheppard

First published in Great Britain in 2019 by:

Young Writers
Remus House
Coltsfoot Drive
Peterborough
PE2 9BF
Telephone: 01733 890066
Website: www.youngwriters.co.uk

Foreword

Dear Reader,

Are you ready to explore the wonderful delights of poetry?

Young Writers' *Poetry Patrol* gang set out to encourage and ignite the imaginations of 5-7 year-olds as they took their first steps into the magical world of poetry. With **Riddling Rabbit, Acrostic Croc** and **Sensory Skunk** on hand to help, children were invited to write an acrostic, sense poem or riddle on any theme, from people to places, animals to objects, food to seasons. *Poetry Patrol* is also a great way to introduce children to the use of poetic expression, including onomatopoeia and similes, repetition and metaphors, acting as stepping stones for their future poetic journey.

All of us here at Young Writers believe in the importance of inspiring young children to produce creative writing, including poetry, and we feel that seeing their own poem in print will keep that creative spirit burning brightly and proudly.

We hope you enjoy reading this wonderful collection as much as we enjoyed reading all the entries.

Contents

Layla-Jo Kitteridge (6)	60		Dallas Taylor (5)	100
K P (6)	61		Raylie Hinks (5)	101
Suhani Gill (6)	62		Tammi-Leigh May (6)	102
Riley Green (7)	63		Olivia Ricketts (7)	103
Ethan Harvey (7)	64		Callum James (6)	104
Rajan Bhamber (7)	65		Mustafah Shabir (6)	105
Finneas Dolan (6)	66		Lily Coles-Mason (5)	106
Freya Jane Underhill (7)	67		Jana Jazaeeri (5)	107
Casey Le'ara Murphy (5)	68		Sudais Farhad (6)	108
Scarlett Leah Mason (6)	69		Ivy-Lee Mason (5)	109
Logan-James Robinson (6)	70		Theo Gray-Milner (5)	110
Roman Sinclair (7)	71		Mackayla Hall (6)	111
Amarveer Singh Khela (5)	72		Ibrahim Ali (5)	112
Danny Hawkes Hoskins (6)	73		Kaiden Hubbard (6)	113
Jake Dennis Curtis (7)	74		Sahil Hussain (5)	114
Viren Ghotra (6)	75		Taneesha Jackson (6)	115
Leo Chinn (6)	76			

Mariam Esa Traore (7) 77
Leila Evelyn Osborne (6) 78
Armaan Rehman (5) 79
Riley Jones (6) 80
Simranjoht Kaur Toor (7) 81
Regan Jones (6) 82
Gurveer Manghra (6) 83
Ewan Roy Tyler-Stevens (6) 84
Muhammad Hassan Hussain (7) 85
Cerys Smith (5) 86

North Walsall Primary Academy, Walsall

Rhia Bansal-Daniel (7) 87
Saafir Sikdar (6) 88
Daniyal Ali (7) 89
Safaa Hussain (6) 90
Maimoona Bibi (7) 91
Zakiyah Ahmed (7) 92
Daniel Perkins (6) 93
Habibah Bibi (7) 94
Ayaan Yasin (6) 95
Eman Ghafoor (5) 96
Aanya Aftkhar (6) 97
Oliver Mayo (6) 98
Laiba Nawaz (6) 99

Oldswinford CE Primary School, Oldswinford

Maisie-Grace Howell (7) 116
Fraser Piers Willetts (6) 118
Sophie Hensman (7) 119
Theo Metaxas (7) 120
Tessa Ayling (7) 121
Noah Dunn (7) 122
Layla Hope Simms (6) 123
Pippa Thompson (6) 124
Holly Jones (7) 125
Seb Roach (6) 126
Eleanor Hadley (6) 127
Freddie Griffiths (6) 128
Maya Mai Warren (6) 129
Annabel Ellis (6) 130
Harriet Turner (6) 131
Phoebe Foxall (6) 132
Rhys Mamoun (6) 133
Ronnie Gould (6) 134
Fynn Clark (6) 135
Marcus Braund (6) 136
Imogen Lewis (7) 137

St Francis Xavier Catholic Primary School, Oldbury

Natalia Wojtowicz (6)	138
Adrienne Bull (5)	139
Imogen Hewitt (6)	140
Brett Lane (5)	141
Ellamae Le-Brown (6)	142
Ronan Woods (5)	143
Guelia Maoso Kumosi (6)	144
Lukasz Andrzej Duniec (5)	145
Skyler Kasaato (5)	146
Erin Ward (5)	147
Jessica Mahoney (6)	148
Joshua Alabi (6)	149
Tiarna Pratley (5)	150
Sienna-Rose Effa Sayers (5)	151
Omhatyo Lewis-Faure (5)	152
Chukwuebuka Attah (5)	153
Alex Mathai (6)	154
James Davis (6)	155

Tenterfields Primary Academy, Tenterfields

Jessie Morgan (5)	156
Tyler James Firth (6)	157
Erin-Jane Elizabeth Griffiths (5)	158
Logan Hickie (6)	159
Molly Rice (6)	160
Evelyn Blackwood (6)	161
Harry Haynes (6)	162
Sienna Multani (6)	163
Tommy Philip Hudson (5)	164
Noah Bubb (6)	165

Whittle Academy, Walsgrave

Emily Mae Jackson (6)	166
Lainey Martin (6)	167
Drishti Dadhich (6)	168
David Ojo (6)	169

The Poems

RIDDLIN' RABBIT

SENSORY SKUNK

ACROSTIC CROC

Who Am I?

I am a toy,
I have a gun,
I have a long hat,
I have a red and white uniform,
I have a black belt,
I am serious,
I have black shoes,
I have a red button,
I am a weapon.
Who am I?

Answer: *The Grand Soldier.*

Nicole Ansere (5)
Barcroft Primary School, Barcroft

Who Am I?

I have a uniform,
I have a red and white t-shirt,
I have a really long hat,
I have two shoes,
I am a toy,
I am serious,
I have a face,
I have a gun,
I have feet.
Who am I?

Answer: A soldier.

Evie-anna Lane (5)
Barcroft Primary School, Barcroft

Who Am I?

I am a toy,
I have a uniform,
I have a gun,
I have gloves,
I am red,
I am wood,
I have black trousers,
I am serious,
I have boots.
Who am I?

Answer: *The Grand Soldier.*

Lotti Harrison (6)
Barcroft Primary School, Barcroft

Who Am I?

I have a uniform with crosses,
I have a gun,
I have dark blue trousers,
I have a bucket-looking hat,
I have polished shoes.
Who am I?

Answer: The Grand Soldier.

Markus Tobias Duckers (6)
Barcroft Primary School, Barcroft

What Am I?

I am a toy,
I have windows,
I am green,
I have passengers,
I have a horn,
I am red,
I am good.
What am I?

Answer: The Grand Express Train.

Arley Benn (5)
Barcroft Primary School, Barcroft

Who Am I?

I have red trousers,
I have peach-coloured skin,
I have a solid helmet,
I have a white moustache.
Who am I?

Answer: *The Old Grand Super Soldier.*

Avneet Bhullar (6)
Barcroft Primary School, Barcroft

What Am I?

I have wheels,
I have a horn,
I have seats,
I am wooden,
I have passengers.
What am I?

Answer: The Grand Express Train.

Tadas Lekavicius (5)
Barcroft Primary School, Barcroft

Who Am I?

I am wood,
I have a long hat,
I have a badge on my hat,
I have a white gun.
Who am I?

Answer: *The Grand Soldier.*

Finlay Williams-McElligott (6)
Barcroft Primary School, Barcroft

What Am I?

I am wooden,
I have wheels,
I have passengers,
I am a toy.
What am I?

Answer: The Grand Express Train.

Ethan Gregory (5)
Barcroft Primary School, Barcroft

What Am I?

I have steam coming out,
I have a chair,
I have passengers.
What am I?

Answer: The Grand Express Train.

Archie Gardiner (5)
Barcroft Primary School, Barcroft

What Am I?

I have wheels,
I have windows,
I have steam,
I have chairs.
What am I?

Answer: A steam train.

Abjot Kaur (6)
Barcroft Primary School, Barcroft

What Am I?

I am wooden,
I have wheels,
I am green.
What am I?

Answer: The Grand Express Train.

Bradley Thomas Dunn (6)
Barcroft Primary School, Barcroft

What Am I?

I have legs,
I am fluffy,
I am cuddly.
What am I?

Answer: The Grand Old Teddy.

Brianna Gooden (6), Yuri, Ekam Singh Badyal & Laural
Barcroft Primary School, Barcroft

Spider

S pinning spider in his web
P lease don't hurt me, I am nice
I ncy Wincy is my name
D angling from a silky thread
E ating flies for my tea
R ound and round I go.

Felix Anyan (5)
Curdworth Primary School, Curdworth

Jungle Adventure

In a dark jungle beneath the tangled
bushes,
I saw a long, scaly, slimy snake.
I quietly tiptoed to have a closer look,
But was startled to see it wide awake.
It was as long as a skipping rope,
With two eyes sparkling like blue marbles.
It looked very fierce, ready to spray venom,
And was hence hiding quietly by the
pebbles.
I turned around and I ran as fast as I could,
But I suddenly fell into the trap,
A kind rat came to rescue me,
And we reached home together with the
help of a map!

Ankush Rag Ananthkumar (7)
Kingswood School, Shirley

Stalker Above The Clouds

I live somewhere really, really high,
Where nobody can see me,
I like travelling around the big round rocks,
I am ugly and green,
My voice is squeaky like a mouse,
Humans are scared of me,
Even though I want to be their friend,
The world seems so harsh on me,
I know I belong somewhere else.
What am I?

Answer: An alien.

Rohan Shoker (7)
Kingswood School, Shirley

Jenna

Jenna is my little sister.
If you blink as she goes past,
you will have missed her.
She is small and very fun
and we like to play in the park.
Sometimes we stay until it's dark.
My favourite is the zip wire,
I climb up onto the tyre
and hold on tight
with all my might,
off I go.
Tally-ho!

Sasha Wallace (7)
Kingswood School, Shirley

A Testing Riddle

I'm great,
I'm sometimes happy,
I'm sometimes sad,
I love explosions,
The things I do are amazing,
I record my work,
I invent in my room,
I make a hypothesis in my book,
I work in a room called a lab,
I like to do experiments.
Who am I?

Answer: A scientist.

Jasmine Bamber (6)
Kingswood School, Shirley

The Snake

We went for a walk,
On our walk we talked,
We came across a snake,
So we called him Jake,
Jake looked like he was in a mood,
Jake was hungry, he needed food,
We thought he escaped from the zoo,
Jake then needed a poo,
We left the snake alone,
So we made our walk home.

Jake Portas (8)
Kingswood School, Shirley

Best Racer!

I live in a burrow
With my friend Murrow,
My ears are long
I can sing a song,
Carrot is my favourite food
I am always in a happy mood,
I like to hop
To reach the top,
I am a little fluffy
And I am so furry.

Who am I?

Answer: A rabbit.

Aadhavan Srinivasan (6)
Kingswood School, Shirley

Hooray Beach Day

B ecome a poet
E very beach day, hip hip hooray
A good beach day today
C hristmas has passed away
H ooray, summer has come today!

D ays are good at the beach
A very good day today
Y ay, hip hip hooray! Time to play!

Alexa Macdonald (6)
Kingswood School, Shirley

Pink Candyfloss

I am like a teddy bear,
I am as tall as a baby tree,
I am fabulous like a peacock,
I am pink like candyfloss,
I am as beautiful as a chick,
I am elegant like a ballerina,
I am a type of bird.
What am I?

Answer: A flamingo.

Veeran Samra (6)
Kingswood School, Shirley

Big And Red

I'm big and red,
I have hoses as part of my body,
I have loud sirens,
I help rescue people from trees,
I can be useful for putting out fires.
What am I?

Answer: A fire engine.

Rhiyan Chatan Chauhan (6)
Kingswood School, Shirley

Food Riddle

People buy me to eat,
But do not eat me,
I am not out of date,
I am hard but not soft,
I come in different shapes and sizes.
What am I?

Answer: A plate.

Katie Cekrezi (6)
Kingswood School, Shirley

The Enormous Bear

B rown like a log from a tree,
E ars that can hear the teeniest mouse
squeaking
A rms that can reach the highest leaves
from a tree
R oars like thunder.

Qasim Khawaja (7)
Kingswood School, Shirley

My Brother And Sister

My brother and sister are a pain in the
bottom,
Although I love them something rotten.

When I'm sad and start to cry,
My sister comes to ask me why.
She puts her arms tight around me,
And says, "Lily, you can have the bendy leg
Barbie."
We go to play until it's late,
We have so much fun, she's my best mate.

My brother's only ten months old,
I love him dearly, let that be told.
He loves to play and shouts my name,
His favourite thing is the crawling game.
We follow him round on our knees,
Until Mommy says, "Stop that please"

She tells us that it's time for bed,
When we will rest our sleepy heads.

We have a story and a kiss goodnight,
Then Mommy turns on our flower night
light,
She kisses us and hugs us tight, then says...
"Love you most my pumpkin, my bean and
my knight."

Lily Rose Alexis Giles (6)
Moat Farm Infant School, Oldbury

Bananas With Apples And Sugar

Bananas and apples mixed together with pears,
Yummy soup with more apples and bananas,
Make it sweet and add more sugar,
But don't add much sugar because it's not healthy,
Add more fruit until it's amazing,
Make letters instead of boring words,
A surprise is coming to you,
So it is a big surprise, just for you!
Bananas and apple are too yummy,
I just think it is the best of any soup,
Pears and sugar,
When you mix it, it tastes the best,
Banana, repeat again,
Every time when we write it,

We love sugar, banana and apple soup,
Soup is the best of all!

Bella Wu (6)
Moat Farm Infant School, Oldbury

Inside Outside

When it's snowing and I'm outside,
I like to have a snowball fight,
When it's snowing and I'm inside,
I like to look at the starlight,
When it's snowing and I'm outside,
I like to think about Miss Nagra,
When it's snowing and I'm inside,
I like to have hot chocolate,
When it's snowing and I'm outside,
I like to make a castle,
When it's snowing and I'm inside,
I like to have pancakes because they are nice.

Bavleen Kaur (6)
Moat Farm Infant School, Oldbury

The Gruffalo

T he animal is fake
H e likes to eat steak
E nchanted woods have a snake.

"G oodbye little mouse," he says
R un away and pay
U npleasant face he has
"F rightfully nice of you," he says
F ish called Tays, he has
A poisonous wart at the end of his nose
L ooking for him, he shouts,
"O h help, oh no! It's a Gruffalo!"

Saubaan Mustafa (6)
Moat Farm Infant School, Oldbury

Your Favourite Person

My person is my family
Because they are always kind to me,
They hug me and they love me,
My baby likes me too,
My baby always smiles and cries
And always helps me with my tricky words,
My dad always plays with me and my baby
at night-time
When he comes back from work,
My mom helps me in my study,
So always respect your family,
I can't live without my family,
I love them forever and ever,
Forever.

Vishavjit Singh Bhuee (6)
Moat Farm Infant School, Oldbury

I Love Eggs

Eggs, eggs, eggs, I love you,
Eggs, eggs, eggs, I swear it's true,
I eat you in the morning when I wake up,
I eat you with soldiers when you're sitting in
a cup.
I love you boiled, especially with your yolk,
Don't burn my toast, that's no joke.
Easter is coming, hip hip hooray,
I get to eat chocolate eggs all day.
Some don't like you, but they are mad,
Without my eggs I'll surely be sad!

Corey Elijah Lal Teji (5)

Moat Farm Infant School, Oldbury

Bella

A small ball of fluff
With stars in her eyes,
Snoozing in her bed
As I walk by,
Small flappy ears,
With fur as black as the night,
She awakens
As I turn on the kitchen light,
She jumps to her feet
With excitement and glee,
Oh no, the kitchen floor!
She's only done a wee!
This is my dog Bella,
Who I love with all my heart,
I would give her anything,
Except for a jam tart.

Ruby Grove (7)
Moat Farm Infant School, Oldbury

A World Of Cars

We use cars for everything,
To drive, to race, to play,
From toys, to real cars, to go-karts,
We use them every day,
We fill them with petrol,
Then go to the station to pay,
After, we drive to work,
And work, work away!
With headlights bright that shine like stars,
And view mirrors that reflect like water,
These fine automobiles are everywhere
As we live in a world of cars.

Umar Mahmood (7)
Moat Farm Infant School, Oldbury

My Family

My little sister Orla loves Peppa Pig,
If she sees a muddy puddle,
She does a big... *splash!*
My aunty Mandy's favourite team is
Liverpool,
They wear a red football kit,
Which I think is pretty cool,
My daddy loves to eat biscuits, treats and
cakes,
We buy them from the shop because he
never bakes,
I love to play my DS game,
I play my mom but she is very lame.

Noah Allen (6)
Moat Farm Infant School, Oldbury

My Favourite Food

My favourite snack is a chicken wrap,
If it is in date it will not snap,
Chicken, lettuce and some sauce too,
Add some cucumber to try something new,
Just thinking about my wrap makes my
tummy rumble,
Mmm, now imagine if we ate it with some
apple crumble,
Now back to my wrap, does it sound
delicious to you?
You want to share? I am sure there is
enough for me and you too.

Jack Bryan Evans (7)
Moat Farm Infant School, Oldbury

Unicorns Love Underpants

U nderpants is what we love

N ot knickers or briefs or anything above

I nside and outside, we wear them every day

C rumbs and dirt, we dust them away

O ver our pants, we wear nothing at all

R eds, greens and blues, large, medium and small

N ever without pants will you see us fly

S unshine has gone now, it is time to say bye.

Lillia Anne Evans (5)

Moat Farm Infant School, Oldbury

World War II

You don't hear advice, just gunshots,
The sun comes up,
The bombs come down,
All I see are bullet holes in the walls,
Like little dots,
I told my mom,
"You can count on me."
I held her hand a little tight,
As I thought of my dad,
In the middle of this war,
Fear, terror and sadness take over me.
Please, please make it stop, Dad.

Isaam Hussain (6)
Moat Farm Infant School, Oldbury

Run From The Roar

Dinosaurs are like dynamite,
They are loud, fiery and can cause a fright,
Some are big and scary,
Some are hairy and wary,
But all could eat you up in one bite,
With their spiky teeth and razor claws,
They could make you wish that you weren't born,
So if you hear a dino roar,
Then run for cover
Before you're in his jaw!

Zane Byrne (6)
Moat Farm Infant School, Oldbury

Everything

A isles in the shops
Y oghurt is perfect for fridges
A nice warm season
N o snow in summer
N ow it is the evening
A pples grow on trees.

T eddies are cuddly toys
E lephants have big ears
J ayan is my big brother
I wrote this poem on the 3rd of February, 2019.

Ayanna Teji (6)
Moat Farm Infant School, Oldbury

Sweet Summer

Summer, summer, come soon,
The sun will shine in the sky,
Stars will twinkle around the moon,
Summer, summer, come soon,
Flowers will bloom,
Bees will be happy to fly around the flowers,
Summer, summer, come soon,
Children will go for rides on their bicycles,
And will enjoy the rainbow in the sky,
Summer, summer, come soon.

Lakhan Johal (6)
Moat Farm Infant School, Oldbury

Minecraft

M ining for shiny diamonds

I ron swords are powerful

N aughty skeletons shoot arrows

E nderdragons are super strong

C hest full of goodies

R ed stone can make machines

A lex fights scary baddies

F riends help each other

T he world of blocks.

Lewis Bellamy (6)

Moat Farm Infant School, Oldbury

My Mother

My mother is my friend,
So dear throughout my life,
You're always near,
You are the sunshine to light my day,
My mum is really great,
She is sweet as can be,
She always takes good care of me,
My mother is the best,
I love you, Mom, forever,
Thanks God for giving me such a great
mum.

Amrit Johal (6)
Moat Farm Infant School, Oldbury

Football

F ootball is my favourite game
O n the pitch, we play
O ver the bar it goes sometimes
T ry to scrore a goal every match
B oots are what we wear on our feet
A goal to win the match
L ots of people cheer us on
L ove the game of football.

Ethan Dwyer (7)
Moat Farm Infant School, Oldbury

A Riddle In Summer

I have two wings,
I am orange and black,
I catch nectar and sweep to the ground,
I find beautiful things and help flowers grow,
I was once ugly, wriggling around,
But now I can fly so high,
I can spin around and twirl upside down.
What am I?

Answer: A butterfly.

Angelee Bhamber (7)
Moat Farm Infant School, Oldbury

Dinosaurs

Dinosaurs, dinosaurs,
Some loved meat,
T-rex, allosaurus and raptors too,
If they were still alive,
They would eat you!

Dinosaurs, dinosaurs,
Some loved plants,
Triceratops, brachiosaurus and stegosaurus too,
If they were still alive,
They wouldn't eat you!

Dawson Brody Vickers (6)
Moat Farm Infant School, Oldbury

Summertime

Summertime, summertime,
I love to play in summertime,
I play in the long grass
And run through the trees,
Smell the flowers
And listen to the bees,
Days out at the beach,
Building castles as high as I can reach,
Splashing around in the sea,
I'm as happy as can be.

Charlie Hughes (7)
Moat Farm Infant School, Oldbury

I Can Be A Friend

I can be a friend by smiling at you,
I can be a friend when you feel blue,
I can be a friend who is funny and kind,
I can be a friend who is there all the time,
I can be a friend when no one wants to,
I can be a friend every single day,
I can be your friend,
So what do you say?

Dougie McLaughlin (5)
Moat Farm Infant School, Oldbury

Winter

Winter, winter, brr it's cold,
Playing in the snow never gets old,
Having fun, so much to explore,
Winter, winter, give us more.

Rain is falling, cold and wet,
My winter raincoat I need to get,
Cold and chilly, snowy and ice,
Everybody knows what winter's like.

Harley Beet (6)
Moat Farm Infant School, Oldbury

Football Match

F lying fast across the pitch

O pen goal

O r over the net

T eams at battle

B oots tied up tight

A ll playing together

L aughing and cheering, just playing the game

L istening for the whistle for the end of match time.

Ralphy Hopton (7)
Moat Farm Infant School, Oldbury

Spring Is Here!

Spring has blossomed on the tree,
Birds are flying happily and free,
The animals come out to play,
Their favourite month is sunny May,
A rabbit is playing down the street,
Eating carrots and broccoli,
I love a spring day
Because March the 15th is my birthday!

Radhiya Kapoor (6)
Moat Farm Infant School, Oldbury

Cyprus

C yprus is my favourite place to visit
Y ellow, golden sun
P laying in the pool with my ball
R esting on the beach in the hot sun
U p, up, up I climb the water slide
S plashing around in the sea, this is my
favourite place to be!

Ethan Towns (5)
Moat Farm Infant School, Oldbury

My Best Friend Spot

When he was a puppy
And I was a baby,
We would share my toast,
When I had a bath,
Spotty used to watch me,
But didn't like it when I splashed the water,
When I had a bedtime story, we would listen
And fall asleep together,
I love my Spotty.

Maddison Firkins-Tandy (5)
Moat Farm Infant School, Oldbury

Unicorns

U nicorns are the best

N ew adventures

I deas to try

C oming high up into the sky

O n and on, up and up

R ide on them and fly in the night sky

N ow you see them

S parkling as they fly.

Evelyn Rose Sullivan (6)
Moat Farm Infant School, Oldbury

Turtle

T ough shell on my back
U nder the water is my home
R oaming around the world for 200 million years
T errific swimmer because of my flippers
L ive for a really long time
E ggs are buried safely in the sand.

Sam Vince (7)
Moat Farm Infant School, Oldbury

Our Dog Jack

We have a dog called Jack,
He likes to eat his food,
When we clap he comes back,
He's a clever little dude.

He likes to go out walking,
And sleeping in his bed,
But most of all, he likes it best
When he's being fed.

Alex Martin Harris (6)
Moat Farm Infant School, Oldbury

The Cat And The Rat

There was a cat who chased a rat,
There was a rat who ran away from a cat,
The cat sat on a mat
And the rat got a pat,
The cat sat in a hat
And the rat found a bat,
The cat and the rat went into a garden
And they both got a snack.

Seren Byrnes (7)
Moat Farm Infant School, Oldbury

Summer Day

I love candyfloss on a summer's day,
It makes my troubles fade away,
I love to play on a summer's day,
With my dolls, while my bunny watches and plays,
I like to play with Lego on a summer's day,
While I watch the day fade away.

Lara-May Vashti-Ann Francis-Jones (6)
Moat Farm Infant School, Oldbury

Monday To Friday

Monday to Friday,
When I'm down and blue,
Our teacher knows just what to do,
With a smile and a nod,
And a, "How'd you do?"
With a smile like hers,
And a laugh so loud,
No wonder she makes all of us proud.

Layla-Jo Kitteridge (6)
Moat Farm Infant School, Oldbury

The Seasons

There are four seasons,
They all have a reason,
When it's winter,
My hands go pinker,
When it's spring,
I hear the birds sing,
When it's summer,
I become a drummer,
When it's autumn,
I eat a plum.

K P (6)
Moat Farm Infant School, Oldbury

Unicorns Love Treats

Unicorns love treats,
They are everywhere,
Unicorns love the outdoors,
Unicorns love treats so yummy,
Unicorns over the rainbow,
If you see a unicorn,
Hide and take a picture,
But if they see you,
They will run away.

Suhani Gill (6)
Moat Farm Infant School, Oldbury

Food

What's your favourite food?
Let me have a guess,
I bet it's sausage rolls,
The pastry is so tasty,
But the sausage is messy,
Today it's super tasty,
So come on everybody,
Let's love sausage rolls together!

Riley Green (7)
Moat Farm Infant School, Oldbury

The Meg

A long time ago,
2.6 million years to be exact,
Lived the largest ever shark,
The megalodon in fact.

Nearly twenty metres long
And with razor teeth,
I would have hated going swimming
In case it lurked beneath.

Ethan Harvey (7)
Moat Farm Infant School, Oldbury

What Am I?

I can fly around,
I have wings,
I am black and yellow,
I make honey,
I am found everywhere except Antarctica,
I come out at springtime,
I make a distinctive sound.
What am I?

Answer: A bee.

Rajan Bhamber (7)
Moat Farm Infant School, Oldbury

Soldier

The soldiers go into battle in their tanks,
They are the heroes,
The ones we all should thank
For protecting us and our country
And for everything they gave,
They deserve their medals
For being so brave.

Finneas Dolan (6)
Moat Farm Infant School, Oldbury

School

S chool is my favourite thing

C lassmates are the best

H ometime makes me sad

O utside play is fun

O tter class is next to mine

L earning is what I do best.

Freya Jane Underhill (7)
Moat Farm Infant School, Oldbury

Space

I went to space in my rocket
To find sweeties in my pocket,
I took a step onto the moon
To find a big red balloon,
I went back in my rocket to stay safe
Because I was all alone in space.

Casey Le'ara Murphy (5)
Moat Farm Infant School, Oldbury

Fred The Elf!

I have an elf who sits on the shelf,
His name is Fred
And his clothes are red.

He goes back to Santa
And says, "Goodbye,
See you next year,
If you are a good boy!"

Scarlett Leah Mason (6)
Moat Farm Infant School, Oldbury

Logan's Poem

Logan is my name,
Football is my favourite game,
The weather I hate is rain,
But I love watching it go down the drain,
I would love to go to Spain
Because we would get to go on a plane.

Logan-James Robinson (6)
Moat Farm Infant School, Oldbury

Sister

S miling every day

I love her very much

S he gives me lots of kisses

T akes all my toys

E nters my room without knocking

R uns around chasing me.

Roman Sinclair (7)
Moat Farm Infant School, Oldbury

Teddy

T eddy is my friend.
E ars are soft and furry.
D id Teddy go to sleep with me?
D o you want to play with me, Teddy?
Y ou are furry and cuddly.

Amarveer Singh Khela (5)
Moat Farm Infant School, Oldbury

The Little Rocket

I'm a little rocket
Pointing to the sky,
It's time to start
My engine and get ready to fly,
When you see my tail fire
I launch into the sky,
Blast off!

Danny Hawkes Hoskins (6)
Moat Farm Infant School, Oldbury

Poppy

Poppy is a dog,
Poppy loves to eat,
Poppy loves to play,
Poppy has soft, white fur,
Poppy has a black nose,
Poppy loves me,
Poppy is my best friend.

Jake Dennis Curtis (7)
Moat Farm Infant School, Oldbury

Diwali

Diwali is the festival of light,
We light candles to make it bright,
We light fireworks and watch them go high,
Then we see them go *boom* up in the sky.

Viren Ghotra (6)
Moat Farm Infant School, Oldbury

Tiger

T eeth big and sharp
I ts head is huge and bold
G rowling scarily
E yes of amber, stripes of black
R unning in the jungle.

Leo Chinn (6)
Moat Farm Infant School, Oldbury

A Special Visitor

I have eight legs like an octopus,
I am black,
I make webs,
I normally make webs on trees or logs.
What am I?

Answer: A spider.

Mariam Esa Traore (7)
Moat Farm Infant School, Oldbury

Bullying Is Bad

Bullying is bad,
Bullying is sad,
Kind is nice,
But that is what's good,
It's happy being nice,
Kind is better,
Bullying is bad.

Leila Evelyn Osborne (6)
Moat Farm Infant School, Oldbury

Sunshine

A hot sunny day in the pool,
A hot sunny day eating ice,
A hot sunny day in the garden,
A hot sunny day on the beach,
A hot sunny day in the park.

Armaan Rehman (5)
Moat Farm Infant School, Oldbury

About Me, Riley Jones

R eading a book
I like jumping on my trampoline
L earning new things
E ating waffles
Y ou help me when I'm sad.

Riley Jones (6)
Moat Farm Infant School, Oldbury

Me On My Hoverboard

I ride my hoverboard day and night,
I go very fast, but not as fast as the speed
of light,
On my hoverboard, I feel free,
As free as a chimpanzee.

Simranjoht Kaur Toor (7)
Moat Farm Infant School, Oldbury

About Me, Regan Jones

R unning around
E ating pancakes
G rapes I love and eating fruit
A rts and crafts I like
N ever giving up.

Regan Jones (6)
Moat Farm Infant School, Oldbury

My Mummy

Never ever fear,
My mummy says, "I'm here!"
She will do
Anything for you,
Now and forever,
She is very clever.

Gurveer Manghra (6)
Moat Farm Infant School, Oldbury

Alpacas

Alpacas have a woolly coat,
It keeps them nice and toasty,
They love to play
With billy goats,
They love to play
All day.

Ewan Roy Tyler-Stevens (6)
Moat Farm Infant School, Oldbury

Tangled Web

I save the world,
I kill the villains,
I use my webs to travel high in the sky.
Who am I?

Answer: Spider-Man.

Muhammad Hassan Hussain (7)
Moat Farm Infant School, Oldbury

Unicorns Love Books

Unicorns love books,
Unicorns love to dance,
Unicorns love to prance,
Unicorns love to fly,
Unicorns love to skip by.

Cerys Smith (5)
Moat Farm Infant School, Oldbury

On My Way To School

On my way to school I saw
A fairy,
A tiny fairy,
A tiny, magical fairy,
A tiny, magical, iridescent fairy,
A tiny, magical, iridescent, elegant fairy,
It made my heart skip a beat.

On my way to school,
I saw a mermaid,
A lovely mermaid,
A lovely, colourful mermaid,
A lovely, colourful, shimmery mermaid,
A lovely, colourful, shimmery, charming
mermaid,
It made me jealous!

Rhia Bansal-Daniel (7)
North Walsall Primary Academy, Walsall

On My Way To School

A fairy,
A tiny fairy,
A tiny, magical fairy,
A tiny, magical, iridescent, elegant fairy,
It made my heart skip a beat.

An alien,
A green alien,
A green, sloppy alien,
A green, sloppy, ugly alien,
A green, sloppy, ugly, squishy alien,
A green, sloppy, ugly, squishy, big alien,
It made me jump out of my skin.

Saafir Sikdar (6)
North Walsall Primary Academy, Walsall

On My Way To School I Saw

A fairy,
A tiny fairy,
A tiny, magical, fairy,
A tiny, magical, iridescent, elegant fairy.

On my way to school, I saw,
Electric Thor,
Electric, handsome Thor,
Handsome, brave, electric Thor,
Handsome, brave, amazing, electric Thor,
He made me jump out of my skin!

Daniyal Ali (7)
North Walsall Primary Academy, Walsall

On My Way To School

On my way to school, I saw
A fairy,
A tiny, magical fairy,
A tiny, iridescent fairy,
It made my heart skip a beat.

On my way to school, I saw
A mermaid,
A magical mermaid,
A magical, tiny, iridescent mermaid,
She made me smile a lot.

Safaa Hussain (6)
North Walsall Primary Academy, Walsall

On My Way To School

I saw a fairy,
A tiny fairy,
A tiny, magical, iridescent fairy,
A tiny, magical, iridescent, elegant fairy,
It made my heart burst.

On my way to school I saw
A brown tree,
A brown, beautiful tree,
A brown, beautiful, large, tree.

Maimoona Bibi (7)
North Walsall Primary Academy, Walsall

On My Way To School I Saw

A fairy,
A tiny fairy,
A tiny, magical, iridescent fairy.

On my way to school, I saw
A tiger,
A big tiger,
A big, orange tiger,
A big, orange, black tiger,
A big, orange, black, beautiful tiger,
It scared me to death!

Zakiyah Ahmed (7)
North Walsall Primary Academy, Walsall

On My Way To School I Saw

A fairy,
A tiny fairy,
A tiny, magic fairy,
A tiny, magical, iridescent fairy.

A green tree,
A leafy tree,
A large tree,
An orange tiger,
A black stripy tiger,
A white stripy tiger.

Daniel Perkins (6)
North Walsall Primary Academy, Walsall

On My Way To School

On my way to school, I saw a fairy,
A tiny fairy,
A tiny, magical fairy,
A tiny, magical, iridescent fairy,
A tiny, magical, iridescent, elegant fairy,
It made my heart skip a beat!

Habibah Bibi (7)
North Walsall Primary Academy, Walsall

Alien

A liens have squishy heads
L ove to eat chocolate cake
I nstead of broccoli
E njoy chocolate cake with sprinkles
N ow they roll to bed.

Ayaan Yasin (6)
North Walsall Primary Academy, Walsall

Alien

A liens small and squishy
L ove to eat cookies
I nstead of fruit and veg
E njoy chocolate cake with sprinkles
N ow they roll to bed!

Eman Ghafoor (5)
North Walsall Primary Academy, Walsall

Aliens

A liens are big and round
L ike a squishy tomato
I found out they have fat tummies
E at lots of food
N ext, they roll over to bed.

Aanya Aftkhar (6)
North Walsall Primary Academy, Walsall

Aliens

A liens have red noses
L ove to eat cake
I nstead of veg and fruit
E njoy strawberry cake with sprinkles
N ow they roll to bed.

Oliver Mayo (6)
North Walsall Primary Academy, Walsall

Aliens

A liens are happy and squishy
L eaving food everywhere
I n the garden eating fruit
E ating Coco Pops
N ow they fall to sleep.

Laiba Nawaz (6)
North Walsall Primary Academy, Walsall

Alien

A liens love underpants

L ove to eat cookies and milk

I nstead of fruit and veg

E njoy chocolate cake

N ow they roll to bed!

Dallas Taylor (5)

North Walsall Primary Academy, Walsall

Alien

A liens are small
L ove to eat cookies
I nstead of fruit and veg
E njoy chocolate cake with sprinkles
N ow they roll to bed!

Raylie Hinks (5)
North Walsall Primary Academy, Walsall

Aliens

A liens are pink and green
L ove to eat vegetables
I nstead of fruit
E at chocolate with ice cream
N ext, they roll to bed.

Tammi-Leigh May (6)
North Walsall Primary Academy, Walsall

On My Way To School

On my way to school,
I saw a zombie,
A green zombie,
A green, bloody zombie,
A green, bloody, ripped zombie,
A green, bloody, ripped, white zombie.

Olivia Ricketts (7)
North Walsall Primary Academy, Walsall

On My Way To School I Saw

A shark,
A sharp shark,
A sharp, blue shark,
A sharp, blue, greedy shark,
A sharp, blue, greedy, scary shark,
It made me jump out of my skin.

Callum James (6)
North Walsall Primary Academy, Walsall

Alien

A liens love underpants
L ove cookies and fruit
I nstead of
E njoying bouncy balls
N ow they go to bed and fall off!

Mustafah Shabir (6)
North Walsall Primary Academy, Walsall

Aliens

A liens are funny and squishy
L ove to eat hot dogs
I nstead of veg
E yes funny and black
N ow they roll off to bed.

Lily Coles-Mason (5)
North Walsall Primary Academy, Walsall

Aliens

A liens like to eat ice cream

L ove to eat pink sprinkles

I nstead of fruit

E njoy lollipops

N ow they roll to bed.

Jana Jazaeeri (5)
North Walsall Primary Academy, Walsall

Aliens

A lien with a pink head
L ove underpants
I nstead of fruit and veg
E njoying chocolate cake
N ow he rolls to bed.

Sudais Farhad (6)
North Walsall Primary Academy, Walsall

Alien

A liens small and squishy
L ove to eat cookies
I nstead of fruit and veg
E njoy chocolate
N ow they roll to bed!

Ivy-Lee Mason (5)
North Walsall Primary Academy, Walsall

Aliens

A liens live in space
L ove chocolate cake
I nstead of salad
E njoy melted chocolate
N ow they fall into bed.

Theo Gray-Milner (5)
North Walsall Primary Academy, Walsall

Alien

A liens round and fat

L ove chocolate cake

I nstead of fruit and salad

E njoy sweets

N ow they fall asleep.

Mackayla Hall (6)
North Walsall Primary Academy, Walsall

Aliens

A liens with big legs
L ove to eat green veg
I nstead of fruit
E yes are big
N ow they roll to bed.

Ibrahim Ali (5)
North Walsall Primary Academy, Walsall

Aliens

A liens want to be big
L ove eating pizza
I nstead of carrots
E njoy playing
N ow roll to bed.

Kaiden Hubbard (6)

North Walsall Primary Academy, Walsall

Aliens

A lien is squishy
L ong legs
I t has big eyes
E njoy chocolate cake
N ow he dashes to bed.

Sahil Hussain (5)

North Walsall Primary Academy, Walsall

On My Way To School I Saw

A fairy,
A tiny fairy,
A tiny, magic fairy,
It made my heart skip a beat.

Taneesha Jackson (6)
North Walsall Primary Academy, Walsall

My Dream

I am rainbow-coloured,
I am sparkly,
I change colours to do with my feelings
And to camouflage,
I like to spend time with my friends and family,
I have a pretty name, Christine,
My best friend has a pretty name, Christella,
I love to meet new people,
I have a swirly horn that is gold, silver and bronze,
I have white and neon-green wings to help me fly,
I love to get dressed up,
I have lots of bows,
My favourite bow is a white bow with pink diamonds,
My favourite birthstone is amethyst because that's my birthstone,

My favourite food is chocolate cake with
jam and pizza,
I don't like noodles or haggis,
I hate lemon drizzle cake because to me it is
sour,
I have a fascinating curly mane and tail,
They are both neon-pink,
I can do tricks like loop-the-loop,
I am independent,
I love to speak different languages,
My rider is called Maisie-Grace.
What am I?

Answer: I am a unicorn.

Maisie-Grace Howell (7)
Oldswinford CE Primary School, Oldswinford

Nature's Home

It is a crisp, cold morning in winter,
Birds fly through the trees, trying not to
catch a splinter,
They are happily looking for food and seed,
Hoping to find lots of juicy berries and nuts
to feed,
Their new little baby birds, all alone, safe
and warm in the nest,
They are snuggled up to their brothers and
sisters to rest,
Robins, magpies, sparrows and blackbirds,
Every morning a familiar sound is heard,
That gently wakes me from my sleep,
Hearing the small, little birds cheep,
They happily sing together a song called the
dawn chorus,
Without a doubt, for the joy and happiness
of all of us.

Fraser Piers Willetts (6)
Oldswinford CE Primary School, Oldswinford

I Want A Pet

I want a pet, I want a pet,
But which one shall I get?
I want a dog, I want a dog,
Not a hamster, a goldfish or a frog,
I'd love a fluffy, cuddly friend,
Who I can play with for hours on end,
We can go for walks over the park,
We'll run and play, laugh and bark,
Coco's the name of my special friend,
Best buds forever, that's the end.

Sophie Hensman (7)
Oldswinford CE Primary School, Oldswinford

Venus Fly Trap

V ivid green leaves
E nticing prey
N ectar sweet like honey
U nkind to flies
S nap! Snap! Snap!

F ierce like a tiger
L aunching like an alligator
Y um! Yum! Yum!

T entacles like an octopus
R ainwater it drinks
A lmost dinner time...
P ounce! Trap! Eat!

Theo Metaxas (7)
Oldswinford CE Primary School, Oldswinford

What Am I?

I live in Antarctica in the South Pole,
I huddle close to others to keep out of the cold,
I like to get fish from the sea to eat,
There are seventeen species of me,
I have black and white feathers which keep me warm,
I have chicks and they are adorable.
What am I?

Answer: A penguin.

Tessa Ayling (7)
Oldswinford CE Primary School, Oldswinford

Rabbit

I'm very fluffy and soft,
I need a lot of space,
I like to hop and jump all over the place,
Around my hutch
And all over your face.

I can be big or small,
Black or white,
My eyes big and bright,
I have big, floppy ears,
That I love you to tickle.

Who am I?

Noah Dunn (7)
Oldswinford CE Primary School, Oldswinford

All Things Magic

I'm magical and beautiful,
I live in an enchanted place,
I'm colours of the rainbow,
I have a pretty mane,
My wings are sparkly
And I have a golden horn,
Jump on my back
And I'll take you to my magical home.
What am I?

Answer: Pegasus the unicorn.

Layla Hope Simms (6)
Oldswinford CE Primary School, Oldswinford

Pets

A nimals come in different types
N ewborn animals are really cute
I love the way guinea pigs squeak
M ice are quiet but I don't know why
A nimals without a home get looked after
L oving people look after pets
S ay that animals are cute!

Pippa Thompson (6)
Oldswinford CE Primary School, Oldswinford

Plastic

P iles of plastic in the water

L ots of sea creatures are in danger

A lways remember to recycle your rubbish

S o many creatures have died from the crime

T onnes of waste thrown away every day

I promise not to litter

C are for our planet.

Holly Jones (7)
Oldswinford CE Primary School, Oldswinford

A Little Riddle

There are a lot of us,
I don't have a lot of hair,
I speak a funny language,
I wear goggles,
Some of us have one eye,
And some of us have two eyes,
I wear blue,
I am yellow,
I love eating bananas.
What am I?

Answer: A Minion.

Seb Roach (6)
Oldswinford CE Primary School, Oldswinford

Dependence

T eamwork makes the dream work
E legant friendship
A wesome manners for friends
M ad friendship for all to share
W orking with close friends
O bviously work with your class
R eunited friends
K eep your friends.

Eleanor Hadley (6)

Oldswinford CE Primary School, Oldswinford

Guess A Dinosaur

I am a dinosaur,
Guess my name if you can.
Unlike the T-Rex, I chew my food,
All I want to eat is plants,
No meat for me.
On my hand I have a thumb spike,
Digging for food, defending myself.
Out with my herd, never alone.
Now can you guess who I am?

Freddie Griffiths (6)
Oldswinford CE Primary School, Oldswinford

A Riddle Of A Fiddle

He is greedy,
He is ginger,
He is fat,
He is stripy,
He is naughty,
He is sometimes angry,
He went to someone's castle,
Someone tried to kill him,
There was another of him.
Who is he?

Answer: Garfield.

Maya Mai Warren (6)
Oldswinford CE Primary School, Oldswinford

The Seasons

Spring is when the daffodils bloom
It feels like new life will arrive soon

Summer is very hot
I like it a lot

Autumn is Halloween
It feels spooky and mean

Winter feels very cold
I want to have someone to hold.

Annabel Ellis (6)
Oldswinford CE Primary School, Oldswinford

Summer At The Seaside

I see soaring seagulls in the bright blue sky,
I hear waves crashing and pebbles spinning,
I taste salty seawater on my lips,
I smell slimy seaweed on the beach,
I feel the hot sun warming my face.

Harriet Turner (6)
Oldswinford CE Primary School, Oldswinford

My Bunny

B unny is nice, bunny is here for me
U ntil my bunny is safe, I look after her
N ow she is inside, she is safe
N ow I will love my bunny forever
Y ou are my favourite.

Phoebe Foxall (6)
Oldswinford CE Primary School, Oldswinford

Dragon Class

There was once a dragon who couldn't fly,
He said, "Mommy, Mommy, please get me
in the sky!"
So he tried and tried
And cried and cried,
He tried one more
And soared and soared.

Rhys Mamoun (6)
Oldswinford CE Primary School, Oldswinford

What Am I?

I'm a bear,
I'm black and white,
I sit down and eat all the time,
I live in a type of forest
And the forests are very big.
What am I?

Answer: I am a panda.

Ronnie Gould (6)
Oldswinford CE Primary School, Oldswinford

Big Dog, Little Dog

I could be big or small,
I'm very fast,
I might chase my ball,
I have a very wet nose,
My nose can smell very good,
I like to doze on my mat.

What am I?

Fynn Clark (6)
Oldswinford CE Primary School, Oldswinford

Hugs

H aving a hug is quite nice,
U nder a blanket having hugs,
G oing for hugs is nice,
S leeping whilst having hugs is nice.

Marcus Braund (6)

Oldswinford CE Primary School, Oldswinford

Love

L oving is caring for others,

O nly your heart will know,

V ery warm feeling,

E veryone should be loved.

Imogen Lewis (7)
Oldswinford CE Primary School, Oldswinford

Winter

W inter has lots of snow
I t's a cold, windy day in winter
N obody is going outside without a coat
T winkle little star is my favourite song
E veryone is happy in my house
R ed, woolly hat and scarves.

Natalia Wojtowicz (6)
St Francis Xavier Catholic Primary School, Oldbury

Winter

W inter is a nice time to spend with your friends

I cy and freezing

N obody leaves the house without a coat

T ea I like in winter

E verybody wears a hat

R ed rubber wellingtons I wear in the snow.

Adrienne Bull (5)

St Francis Xavier Catholic Primary School, Oldbury

Winter

W inter is my favourite time of year
I n winter we go outside to play
N obody goes outside without a hat
T o go out, we need a sledge
E very day icicles fall down
R eal snow is falling down.

Imogen Hewitt (6)

St Francis Xavier Catholic Primary School, Oldbury

Winter

W inter is very nice

I ce is very cold

N obody goes out of their homes

T ents aren't very warm in winter

I n winter everything is very cold

R ain makes the snow disappear.

Brett Lane (5)
St Francis Xavier Catholic Primary School, Oldbury

Winter

W inter is cold and icy
  I n winter it's icy and cold on the door
N othing makes us warm
 T ime to play with the snow
E verybody likes snow
R eally fun to play in the snow.

Ellamae Le-Brown (6)
St Francis Xavier Catholic Primary School, Oldbury

Winter

W onderful winter walks

I t is chilly in winter

N ecks, scarves and hoods

T rees lose every single leaf

E verybody likes snow in winter

R acing in the snow is exciting.

Ronan Woods (5)

St Francis Xavier Catholic Primary School, Oldbury

Winter

W e went out in the snow and rode a sledge
 I 'm so cold in the snow
N ow I like snow, it is fun
T oday it is cold
E verybody likes winter
R eally cold in the snow.

Guelia Maoso Kumosi (6)
St Francis Xavier Catholic Primary School, Oldbury

Winter

W andering around in the snow
 I t's a windy time to drink cocoa
N ice walk in the snow
T emperatures in the tens
E njoying hot cocoa
R ain makes snow vanish.

Lukasz Andrzej Duniec (5)
St Francis Xavier Catholic Primary School, Oldbury

Winter

W inter is before spring
I t is a nice day
N obody likes snow
T he temperature in winter is very low
E verybody thinks they are Elsa
R unning home to get warm.

Skyler Kasaato (5)
St Francis Xavier Catholic Primary School, Oldbury

Winter

W inter has lots of snow

I t was so cold

N obody leaves without their coats

T oo cold

E lsa loves snow

R eady to play in the snow.

Erin Ward (5)

St Francis Xavier Catholic Primary School, Oldbury

Winter

W inter is cold
  I cicles drop water
N othing was on the ground
T oday it snowed
E xpect more snow
R eady to play in the snow.

Jessica Mahoney (6)
St Francis Xavier Catholic Primary School, Oldbury

Winter

W inter walks are a battle
  I like the snow
N othing but snow
T oday is cold
E xtra cold today
R osy red warm blanket.

Joshua Alabi (6)
St Francis Xavier Catholic Primary School, Oldbury

Winter

W inter is fun
  I ce makes it slippy
N ice day
T he boy went sledging
E nters his warm house
R eady to sleep.

Tiarna Pratley (5)
St Francis Xavier Catholic Primary School, Oldbury

Winter

W inter is snow

I ce is cold

N ice hot cocoa

T he white snow

E verybody plays together

R unning in the rain.

Sienna-Rose Effa Sayers (5)
St Francis Xavier Catholic Primary School, Oldbury

Winter

W inter
I like to play in the snow
N ice
T eachers like snow days
E verybody has fun
R unning in the snow.

Omhatyo Lewis-Faure (5)
St Francis Xavier Catholic Primary School, Oldbury

Winter

W inter is nice

I love cocoa

N ice day

T he white snow

E nter my warm house

R eady to throw snowballs.

Chukwuebuka Attah (5)

St Francis Xavier Catholic Primary School, Oldbury

Winter

W hat I like is snow
I love hot cocoa
N o school
T he snow was so cold
E lsa
R eady to play.

Alex Mathai (6)
St Francis Xavier Catholic Primary School, Oldbury

Winter

W inter

I ncredible

N ice

T hrowing snowballs

E lsa

R unning and playing.

James Davis (6)

St Francis Xavier Catholic Primary School, Oldbury

Elephants

E lephants are my favourite animal
L ittle elephants hold their mummy's tails with their trunks
E lephants have grey skin
P eople can ride elephants
H ungry elephants eat grass
A group of elephants is a herd
N oisy elephants blow their trunks like trumpets
T heir tusks are made of ivory
S ome elephants do tricks at the circus.

Jessie Morgan (5)
Tenterfields Primary Academy, Tenterfields

The Shark

There was a shark called Marvin,
He was always starving,
He was ferocious and had sharp teeth,
His gums were pink underneath,
He wanted to catch and eat all the fish,
He thought they would make a tasty dish,
The fish were clever and all swam close together,
So the shark could not catch them
And he was mad forever.

Tyler James Firth (6)
Tenterfields Primary Academy, Tenterfields

My Life

E verybody has to be nice
R eece is my big brother
I love my mommy and daddy lots and lots
N anny Jane gives me treats.

J une is the month of my birthday
A lways be loving and caring
N anny Julie gives me ice cream &
chocolate sauce
E rin-Jane is my name!

Erin-Jane Elizabeth Griffiths (5)
Tenterfields Primary Academy, Tenterfields

Best Day Of The Year

B irthday presents to unwrap

I nvite all of my friends

R eally yummy cake

T ime to blow out the candles

H appy birthday to me

D isco lights and dancing

A day to celebrate

Y ippee!

Logan Hickie (6)
Tenterfields Primary Academy, Tenterfields

Underwater Beauty

My golden hair shines bright at night,
My flowing tail shimmers at night,
My voice is colourful, air swaying,
My beautiful blue eyes wave,
When the waves are wavy.
Who am I?

Answer: A mermaid.

Molly Rice (6)
Tenterfields Primary Academy, Tenterfields

What Am I?

I have four legs
I have soft, silky fur
I purr when I dance about
I have four paws
I have two sparkly, pointy ears
I have a rainbow, magical horn
What am I?

Answer: A unicorn cat.

Evelyn Blackwood (6)
Tenterfields Primary Academy, Tenterfields

Our Cat

Our cat went to the flat
And sat on a mat,
Our cat met a rat
And he was very fat,
Our cat was a bit silly
And his friend was called Billy,
We love our cat,
Even when he chases bats.

Harry Haynes (6)
Tenterfields Primary Academy, Tenterfields

Oi Dog

The dog sat on the frog,
The frog said to the dog,
"From now on, dogs should sit on logs,
Cats should sit on mats,
Whales should sit on nails,
Frogs should sit on dogs."

Sienna Multani (6)
Tenterfields Primary Academy, Tenterfields

The Bear

The bear went to his lair,
All his family were there,
His children were in bed,
Their pyjamas were red,
They said, "Hello Dad, we are glad you're okay."

Tommy Philip Hudson (5)
Tenterfields Primary Academy, Tenterfields

Dinosaur Claws

Dinosaurs had razor claws,
They talked with really loud roars,
The biggest ones were very strong,
Their tails were scary and incredibly long.

Noah Bubb (6)
Tenterfields Primary Academy, Tenterfields

Artist Dream

Every day I like to look into an artist's book
To find which paintings I can see
And imagine what an artist I can be.

I fetch my paper, paint and brush,
But take my time not to rush.

I splish and splosh and paint the sun
And add a playground that looks so fun,
Children can play there all day long
And I finish my painting while singing a
song.

Emily Mae Jackson (6)
Whittle Academy, Walsgrave

Summer Riddle

I like to wear a yellow top with my favourite
blue jeans,
I wear a summer hat,
Then I sit on the warm silver sand,
I have long golden hair,
I have children whose names are James,
Sally and Awaker.
Who am I?

Answer: I'm Mum in summer.

Lainey Martin (6)
Whittle Academy, Walsgrave

Little Penguin

I am a little penguin
In the snow,
I slide on my tummy,
To and fro,
I eat the fish
From the deep blue sea,
I am black and white,
As you can see.

Drishti Dadhich (6)
Whittle Academy, Walsgrave

Snakes In The Jungle

Snakes behind your back wall,
You are looking at other animals,
The snake's still behind your back,
While you are looking at the patterns.

David Ojo (6)
Whittle Academy, Walsgrave

Young Writers Information

We hope you have enjoyed reading this book – and that you will continue to in the coming years.

If you're a young writer who enjoys reading and creative writing, or the parent of an enthusiastic poet or story writer, do visit our website **www.youngwriters.co.uk**. Here you will find free competitions, workshops and games, as well as recommended reads, a poetry glossary and our blog.

If you would like to order further copies of this book, or any of our other titles, then please give us a call or visit **www.youngwriters.co.uk**.

Young Writers
Remus House
Coltsfoot Drive
Peterborough
PE2 9BF
(01733) 890066
info@youngwriters.co.uk

 @YoungWritersUK @YoungWritersCW